Where You DARE Not Go

Morbid Metropolis

SCARY STORIES OF THE CITY

by
Natalie Lunis, Joyce Markovics,
and Dinah Williams

Minneapolis, Minnesota

Credits
Cover and title page, © SeanPavonePhoto/Adobe Stock and © haeton/Adobe Stock and © Rixie/Adobe Stock; 4–5, © IM_photo/Shutterstock and © Artranq/Adobe Stock and © Vladimir Arndt/Adobe Stock; 6, © Konstantin Sutyagin/Adobe Stock; 7TR, © James Zeruk, Jr./Wikimedia; 7BR, © ysbrandcosijn/Adobe Stock and © toshihiro emi/Adobe Stock; 8, © Ajay Suresh/Wikimedia; 9BL, © Library of Congress; 10ML, © assetseller/Adobe Stock; 10, © Bettmann Archive/Getty Images; 11TR, © Niday Picture Library/Alamy Stock Photo; 12, © Steve Cukrov/Shutterstock; 13TR, © Lustre Art Group/Adobe Stock; 13BL, © Denis Aglichev/Adobe Stock; 14, © Ajay Suresh/Wikimedia; 15TR, © Vinnie Zuffante/Getty Images; 16, © drnadig/iStock photo; 17MR, © Alexey Kuznetsov/Adobe Stock; 17BL, © santiago/Adobe Stock; 18, © jkbeachtour/Shutterstock; 19TR, © Public domain/Wikimedia; 19BL, © ivgaphotographer/Shutterstock; 20, © Public domain/Wikimedia; 21MR, © Warpedgalerie/Adobe Stock; 22, © Studio Melange/Adobe Stock; 23TR, © Alpha Historica/Alamy Stock Photo; 24, © Barry King/Alamy Stock Photo; 25TR, © Everett Collection/Shutterstock; 26, © debra millet/Shutterstock; 27TR, © Public domain/Wikimedia; 27B, © thomas/Adobe Stock; 28, © Orhan Cam/Shutterstock; 29TR, © Payton Chung/Wikimedia; 30, © Alex Millauer/Shutterstock; 31BL, © Masheter Movie Archive/Alamy Stock Photo; 32, © marchello74/Adobe Stock; 33BR, © Matthew Lapiska/NYC DDC; 34, © Laura/Adobe Stock; 35TR, © Public domain/Wikimedia; 35MR, © Public domain/Wikimedia; 36, © Hulton Archive/ Getty Images; 37TR, © Public domain/Wikimedia; 38, © Fernando Garcia Esteban/Shutterstock; 39BR, © Benjamin Clapp/Shutterstock; 40, © Public domain/Wikimedia; 41TR, © Public domain/Wikimedia; 42–43, © Triff/Shutterstock and © Svnova/Shutterstock

Bearport Publishing Company Product Development Team
Publisher: Jen Jenson; Director of Product Development: Spencer Brinker; Managing Editor: Allison Juda; Editor: Cole Nelson; Associate Editor: Naomi Reich; Associate Editor: Tiana Tran; Designer: Kim Jones; Designer: Kayla Eggert; Designer: Steve Scheluchin; Production Specialist: Owen Hamlin

Statement on Usage of Generative Artificial Intelligence
Bearport Publishing remains committed to publishing high-quality nonfiction books. Therefore, we restrict the use of generative AI to ensure accuracy of all text and visual components pertaining to a book's subject. See BearportPublishing.com for details.

Library of Congress Cataloging-in-Publication Data is available at www.loc.gov or upon request from the publisher.

ISBN: 979-8-89577-094-8 (hardcover)
ISBN: 979-8-89577-211-9 (ebook)

Copyright © 2026 Bearport Publishing Company. All rights reserved. No part of this publication may be reproduced in whole or in part, stored in any retrieval system, or transmitted in any form or by any means, electronic, mechanical, photocopying, recording, or otherwise, without written permission from the publisher. Bearport Publishing is a division of FlutterBee Education Group.

For more information, write to Bearport Publishing, 5357 Penn Avenue South, Minneapolis, MN 55419.

Contents

Haunted Streets 4
Broken Dreams 6
A Deadly Dwelling 8
Lincoln Ghosts 10
Moviegoing Ghosts 12
A Lingering Spirit 14
Unfinished Work 16
Cursed Ground 18
An Eerie Inn 20
The Library Ghost 22
Escape from Death 24
The Belasco Theatre Ghost 26
Washington's Most Haunted 28
Haunted House of Wax 30
Thousands of Corpses 32
A Star-Spangled Ghost 34
Phantom Stage 36
The Lady of the Lake 38
Home, Sweet Home 40

Three Morbid Metropolises 42
Glossary 44
Read More 46
Learn More Online 46
Index 47

Haunted Streets

Cities are home to millions of people, all going about their everyday lives. But what happens in cities when the lives of those long dead can still be seen? Are New York City, Washington, D.C., and Los Angeles looking toward the future? Or is the past still holding on in a haunting way?

Broken Dreams

THE HOLLYWOOD SIGN
LOS ANGELES, CALIFORNIA

The Hollywood sign is as famous as some of the town's celebrities. To many people, it marks a place where dreams come true. Yet for one struggling actress, it was the spot where the hopes of a lifetime ended.

The Hollywood sign

By 1978, the Hollywood sign was old and worn out. The letters were torn down to make way for a new version made from materials that would last longer. Now, just as before, the letters can be seen for miles.

Made up of letters that are 45 feet (14 m) tall, the Hollywood sign sits high atop a hill. It was created in 1923 to advertise a community of homes for sale named Hollywoodland. Twenty-six years later, in 1949, city officials dropped the word *land*. Now spelling out *Hollywood*, the sign reminded all those who saw it of the glitter and promise of the world-famous movie industry.

Peg Entwistle

Yet the sign has also been a place of sadness and death. In 1932, a young actor named Peg Entwistle was upset because she could not find work in the movies. On September 16, she left her uncle's small Hollywood home and headed toward the sign. Once there, she climbed a construction ladder and jumped to her death from the top of the letter H.

Since that terrible day, Entwistle's ghost has been seen haunting the hill, which is now a park. Park rangers and visitors have spotted her in the form of a blonde woman in 1930s clothing, most often when it is foggy. Some have also noticed the smell of gardenias—the scent found in Entwistle's favorite perfume.

7

A Deadly Dwelling

THE HOUSE OF DEATH
NEW YORK, NEW YORK

The House of Death has earned its horrifying name over many decades. The brownstone, built in 1856, is considered to be one of the most haunted places in Manhattan—and an undeniable den of death.

The House of Death

Soon after the actor Jan Bryant Bartell and her husband moved into the old building in 1957, strange things began to happen. At first, the actor felt an unusual chill in the air. Then, more unnerving things began to occur.

One day, she felt something brush against the back of her neck, but when she whipped around to look, nothing was there. She also heard mysterious footsteps and loud crashing sounds. Sometimes, she smelled the odor of something rotten. Most terrifying of all was what Bartell described as a monstrous moving shadow that crept up behind her.

After years of spooky encounters, Bartell hired a paranormal expert to help rid the building of ghosts. Once in the house, the expert felt his body become possessed by one of the spirits, who said it would never leave the building! That's when the actor and her husband decided to move out. However, Bartell felt that she never truly left the House of Death behind—she was haunted by memories of it until her death in 1973.

Author Mark Twain in 1901

The famous writer Samuel Clemens, also known as Mark Twain, lived in the house from 1900 to 1901. Long after he died, one of the building's residents found a visitor in her living room. The shocked woman asked the man what he was doing. He replied, "My name is Clemens . . ." Then he vanished!

Lincoln Ghosts

LINCOLN BEDROOM, THE WHITE HOUSE
WASHINGTON, D.C.

The White House is the home of the United States' elected leader—the president. For this reason, it is sometimes called the people's house. Should it also be called the people's *haunted* house? After all, many ghosts are said to be found there.

The Lincoln Bedroom

The White House

The most famous ghosts to haunt the White House belong to the Lincoln family. In the winter of 1862, while Abraham Lincoln was serving as president, his 11-year-old son Willie became ill with typhoid and died shortly afterward. Both President Lincoln and his wife, Mary, were filled with grief. Mary, who had a strong belief in spirits, soon arranged several séances so she could try to contact her son. Less than a year later, she began to see him at night, standing at the foot of her bed.

Willie Lincoln

In April 1865, about three years after Willie's death, President Lincoln was shot and killed while attending a play at Ford's Theatre in downtown Washington, D.C. Since then, his ghost has been seen inside the White House many times. Most often, it is spotted in a room that was once Lincoln's office.

Years after Lincoln's death, a bed and other pieces of furniture belonging to the Lincolns were brought into Lincoln's old office. The room became known from that time on as the Lincoln Bedroom. It was a place for very important guests and—according to some visitors—one very important presidential ghost.

During the 1940s, British Prime Minister Winston Churchill visited the White House and stayed in the Lincoln Bedroom. According to reports, he saw Lincoln's ghost standing near the fireplace. After that, he asked to be moved to another room.

Moviegoing Ghosts

THE VOGUE THEATRE
HOLLYWOOD, CALIFORNIA

In the old days, when people in Hollywood went to the movies, they often went to the Vogue Theatre. For more than 60 years, they lined up there to see films made at nearby studios. Once inside, many reportedly saw ghosts as well.

The Vogue Theatre

The Vogue Theatre closed in the early 1990s. Today, the building is used for musical performances and other kinds of entertainment. The ghosts from the movie theater have not reappeared—so far.

People say that before the Vogue Theatre was built in 1935, Prospect Elementary School stood on the same spot. In 1901, a raging fire burned the building to the ground. Twenty-five students were killed, along with their teacher, Miss Elizabeth.

Over the years, many moviegoers inside the Vogue reported seeing the ghosts of children as well as Miss Elizabeth. The spirit of one girl liked to skip up and down the aisle during movies. She came around so often that many people working at the theater received complaints.

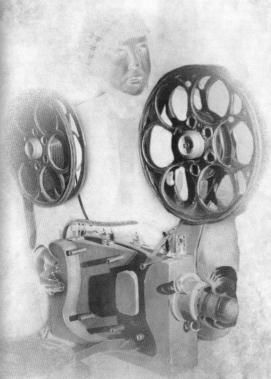

Later, another ghost began to make appearances. People have identified him as Fritz, a movie projectionist who worked at the Vogue for nearly 40 years and died of a heart attack in the projection booth. According to some, his spirit would change the film reels if the projectionist who was working that day fell asleep on the job.

A Lingering Spirit

THE DAKOTA
NEW YORK, NEW YORK

The Dakota is a lavish apartment building near Central Park. Built in the 1880s, this famous building is home to the rich and famous . . . and, some say, the dead and buried.

The Dakota

One of the Dakota's most famous residents was the rock and roll musician John Lennon. He moved into the large building with his wife, Yoko Ono, in 1973. From the beginning, there were spooky stirrings in the building. For example, one day Lennon saw a wispy figure of a woman floating in the hallway. Other residents experienced peculiar things as well. There were reports of unexplained footsteps. Sometimes, rugs and chairs were said to slide across the floors on their own. However, a truly horrific thing happened in 1980.

Yoko Ono and John Lennon outside The Dakota

On December 8, 1980, Lennon and Ono were returning to their apartment when a strange man holding a gun appeared. The crazed fan shot Lennon in the back four times. Lennon died soon after.

After his death, Ono saw Lennon sitting at his piano in their apartment. He turned to her and said, "Don't be afraid. I'm still with you." In 1983, a neighbor reported seeing Lennon near the entrance of the Dakota. He claims that Lennon was "surrounded by an eerie light."

John Lennon was a member of The Beatles, a world-famous band.

Unfinished Work

UNITED STATES CAPITOL
WASHINGTON, D.C.

Located atop a hill near the center of Washington, D.C., the United States Capitol is one of the city's most important buildings. It is where members of both the United States Senate and House of Representatives meet. These people who make the country's laws may not be the only ones who show up for work there, however. Reportedly, the ghosts of some who first built the Capitol do as well.

The United States Capitol

Work on the United States Capitol began in 1793, while George Washington was president. In later years, parts of the building were redesigned and rebuilt, resulting in the building's current appearance. In its center is a huge dome. To the sides of the dome are two main wings, or sections. One is known as the Senate wing, and the other is known as the House of Representatives wing.

According to legend, a stonemason was killed during the earliest construction of what is now the Senate wing. One version of the story says that he was crushed to death when a wall collapsed and buried him. Another says that he got into an argument with a fellow worker and was killed when the man hit him over the head with a brick. Whether he was the victim of an accident or a murder, some say the stonemason has remained in the basement ever since. He is sometimes heard banging and scratching from behind a wall. At other times, his ghostly figure is seen passing through it.

Pierre Charles L'Enfant was a French engineer hired by George Washington to design plans for the Capitol and other parts of Washington, D.C. Some say he was never paid for his work, however. Since his death, his ghost has reportedly been seen angrily rushing through the hallways of the Capitol, with the plans he drew up under his arm.

Cursed Ground

GRIFFITH PARK
LOS ANGELES, CALIFORNIA

Griffith Park is one of the largest and most famous city parks in the world. It has been used as an outdoor location for many film shoots, and it is home to the Hollywood sign. If the stories people tell are true, it is also home to an angry ghost.

Griffith Park

The land that is now Griffith Park was once owned by a wealthy man named Don Antonio Feliz. In 1863, he died suddenly from smallpox. According to legend, while lying on his deathbed, he was tricked into leaving his property to another wealthy landowner. Furious over losing her inheritance, Feliz's 17-year-old niece, Doña Petronilla, put a curse on the land.

Griffith J. Griffith

Nineteen years later, in 1882, a millionaire named Griffith J. Griffith bought the cursed land. In 1891, he was shot and wounded by a business rival. Five years later, he donated 3,105 acres (1,257 ha) to be used as a park. Still, he could not escape the curse. In 1903, he went to prison for shooting and badly injuring his wife.

Several ghosts have been spotted in the park Griffith left behind. The most famous is that of Doña Petronilla. Most often, she haunts the park's trails on horseback, wearing a white dress. She has also been seen on dark, rainy nights in the Paco Feliz Adobe, the oldest structure in the park.

Two other ghostly horseback riders have been reported in Griffith Park as well. One is believed to be Don Antonio Feliz. The other is said to be the spirit of Griffith J. Griffith.

An Eerie Inn

THE EAR INN
NEW YORK, NEW YORK

Less than two blocks from the Hudson River in downtown Manhattan is the Ear Inn. The nineteenth-century house has a long history. It's also the favorite hangout of a spooky sailor.

The Ear Inn

The brick town house was originally built in 1817 as a home for a shop owner named James Brown. In 1833, Brown sold the house, and it became a pub. Sailors—and, occasionally, pirates who robbed ships on the Hudson River—went to the pub for a drink.

According to legend, an old sailor named Mickey was killed in front of the pub, and many believe his spirit still haunts his favorite hangout. People say they know Mickey is around when the fireplace bursts into flames on its own. Sometimes, people sitting at the bar notice their drinks mysteriously emptying.

In September 2014, a server and her friend were napping upstairs at the Ear Inn. The server awoke to find her friend staring into space. When she asked him what he was doing, the friend replied, "I'm just saying hello to the strange man standing in the corner." No one was there.

It's believed that James Brown fought in the American Revolution (1775–1783) and worked for George Washington.

The Library Ghost

LIBRARY OF CONGRESS
WASHINGTON, D.C.

Located just east of the United States Capitol is the Library of Congress, where one of the world's largest collections of printed books—as well as letters, pictures, and maps—can be found. In addition, a worried ghost is said to walk among these important items. What is he searching for . . . and why?

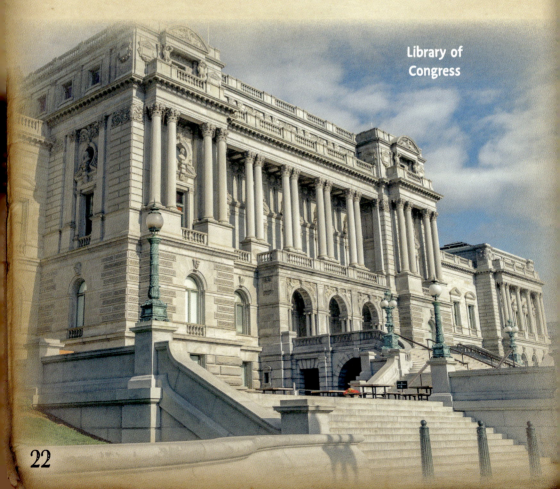

Library of Congress

The Library of Congress was started in 1800. Its main purpose was to provide information to members of the United States government. At first, the library's collection was kept in a room in the Capitol building. As the collection grew bigger and bigger, three separate buildings, one next to the other, were constructed to hold it.

Inside the old Library of Congress

According to legend, a worker from the early days of the library did not trust banks. As a result, he hid thousands of dollars between the pages of some of the books. Unfortunately, he died before he could get the money back and spend it, and since his death, he has returned as a ghost to look for it. Some versions of the story say that he's been spotted in the library's old location in the Capitol building. Other versions say that he haunts the new library, forever opening and flipping through books in search of his lost, hidden money.

Sightings of a ghost wearing a police officer's uniform have been reported in the new Library of Congress. The spirit is a helpful one as he is said to guide people when they become lost among the miles of books stacked on shelves.

Escape from Death

HARRY HOUDINI'S HOME
LOS ANGELES, CALIFORNIA

In 1926, when Harry Houdini died suddenly at age 52, he was one of the most famous men in the world. An escape artist and magician, Houdini amazed audiences by seeming to do the impossible. Was he also able to return from the dead and visit an estate in the Hollywood Hills where he had once lived?

The estate where Houdini lived

Houdini stayed at the estate when he came to Hollywood to make movies. His movies were not nearly as successful as his performances onstage, however, and they did not earn much money.

Throughout the early 1900s, Harry Houdini thrilled audiences. He escaped from being buried alive, chained up and dunked in water, and suspended high in the air with his arms tightly wrapped. Of course these tricks weren't really brought about by magic. Instead, they were the result of great physical skill and many hours of practice. Yet some say Houdini did believe in the supernatural—especially in the possibility of contacting the dead.

Harry and Bess Houdini

During his marriage, Houdini made an agreement with his wife, Bess. When one of them died, the two would try to communicate with each other. After Houdini's death, Bess held many séances at an estate overlooking Hollywood where she and Houdini had lived in the 1920s and early 1930s.

The séances were never successful, but still, the famous escape artist may have managed to come back on his own. Sixteen years after Bess's death, the estate's beautiful main house burned down. Since then, many claim to have seen Houdini's dark figure walking among its ruins. Often, the ghostly shape has been spotted on a stone staircase in the garden.

The Belasco Theatre Ghost

THE BELASCO THEATRE
NEW YORK, NEW YORK

Broadway is home to some of the world's most famous theaters. When the curtain drops at the Belasco Theatre on West 44th Street, that's when a ghostly performance begins.

The Belasco Theatre

The top floor of the Belasco Theatre used to be the home of the theater's founder, David Belasco, who died almost 100 years ago. Sometimes, one of the theater's managers hears something strange coming from the locked top floor. It's the unmistakable sound of footsteps. . . .

David Belasco

David Belasco was born in 1853 and devoted his life to the theater. He wrote and directed plays and launched the careers of many young actors. After he died in 1931, actors recalled seeing a dark figure on the balcony after a performance. Sometimes, the figure would even come up to them and shake their hands.

One night more recently, an usher working in the lobby jokingly yelled out, "Good night, Mr. Belasco." Suddenly, all the lobby doors swung open at the same time! Chills went up and down the usher's spine. Soon after, the terrified woman quit her job and vowed never to return to the Belasco.

It was reported that an old caretaker's dog used to growl at an unseeen intruder every day at 4:00 p.m. People wondered whether the dog could see Mr. Belasco's spirit.

Washington's Most Haunted

THE OCTAGON HOUSE
WASHINGTON, D.C.

The word *octagon* means eight sides. Yet the 200-year-old Octagon House, located in the same Washington neighborhood as the White House, actually has just six sides. That's not the only strange thing about it, however. It is also known as the most haunted house in the city.

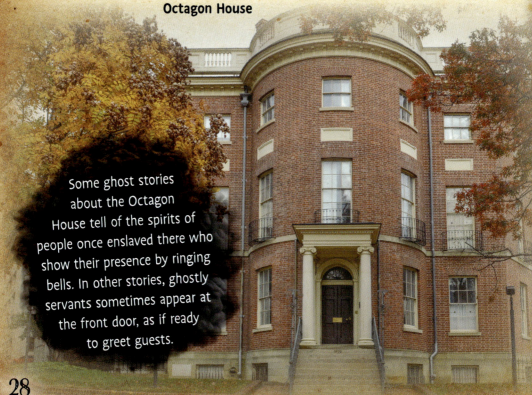

Octagon House

Some ghost stories about the Octagon House tell of the spirits of people once enslaved there who show their presence by ringing bells. In other stories, ghostly servants sometimes appear at the front door, as if ready to greet guests.

The Octagon House was built in 1801. Its first owner, Colonel John Tayloe III, was a wealthy Virginia landowner who was friendly with many American leaders, including George Washington. One day, however, Tayloe learned that his daughter had fallen in love with and planned to marry a young British officer. Like most Americans at the time, Tayloe considered the British to be enemies, so he was completely against the marriage. During an argument about it, his daughter became terribly upset and fell from the top of the house's beautiful spiral staircase. She died as a result.

The staircase inside the Octagon House

Shockingly, a similar event occurred a few years later. Another of Tayloe's daughters had married a man whom the colonel did not like. When she returned home to try to make peace with the family, she too fell to her death from the top of the stairs.

Following the two tragedies, strange sights and sounds have been reported. Some people have seen a faint light traveling up the stairs, as if a candle is being carried by an unseen person. Others have heard a scream or a thud before spotting a crumpled body on the floor just below the last step.

Haunted House of Wax

HOLLYWOOD WAX MUSEUM
LOS ANGELES, CALIFORNIA

For more than 50 years, tourists have visited the Hollywood Wax Museum. This unusual attraction—filled with life-size figures of famous stars—is open until midnight most evenings. On some dark nights, however, visitors have seen much more than just their favorite celebrities.

Hollywood Wax Museum

The Hollywood Wax Museum contains wax figures of hundreds of actors—many of them dressed in the costumes they wore in their best-known movies. As visitors walk through darkened rooms, they can see Marilyn Monroe, Charlie Chaplin, Angelina Jolie, Samuel L. Jackson, and other big names from both the past and the present. When they enter a special section called the Horror Chamber, visitors come upon such classic movie monsters as Dracula, Frankenstein, and the Phantom of the Opera.

Not surprisingly, many people find the museum and its lifelike wax figures spooky. Yet there is another reason why being inside the wax museum sends a chill down visitors' spines. When people take photos with the figures at night, something odd is said to happen. Instead of wax figures, strange colored shapes often appear in the photos. A few visitors even claim to have actually seen ghosts moving among the displays.

Vincent Price in *House of Wax*

The Horror Chamber includes a wax figure of actor Vincent Price from the 1953 movie *House of Wax*. In this horror film, he plays the owner of a wax museum who kills people so that he can use their bodies to make life-size figures that will last forever.

31

Thousands of Corpses

WASHINGTON SQUARE PARK
NEW YORK, NEW YORK

Washington Square Park is a lovely place to take a stroll. There's a large fountain, places to picnic, and a beautiful archway. What some visitors don't know, however, is that the park sits on top of a mass grave!

Washington Square Park

The land that makes up Washington Square Park was used as a cemetery from 1797 to 1826.

In 1797, the City of New York created a public burial ground, or potter's field, in the area that's now Washington Square Park. Poor people, criminals, and victims of deadly diseases were buried there in large graves. Sometimes, the bodies were put in wooden coffins and then placed into a large hole. Most often, however, the corpses were simply dumped into the ground.

In the late 1700s and early 1800s, there was an outbreak of yellow fever in the city. It claimed the lives of thousands. Many of those who died were laid to rest in the potter's field. In 1827, the mass grave was turned into a public square, and later, a park. People quickly forgot about Washington Square's grim past.

In 2015, city workers digging in the park made a stunning discovery. They found an underground chamber filled with skeletons and coffins! Some experts believe that as many as 20,000 corpses are still buried beneath the park.

The chamber below Washington Square Park

A Star-Spangled Ghost

THE FRANCIS SCOTT KEY HOUSE AND BRIDGE
WASHINGTON, D.C.

As the writer of the lyrics of "The Star-Spangled Banner," Francis Scott Key lives on through his famous song. Some people say he also lives on as a ghost in his old Washington neighborhood.

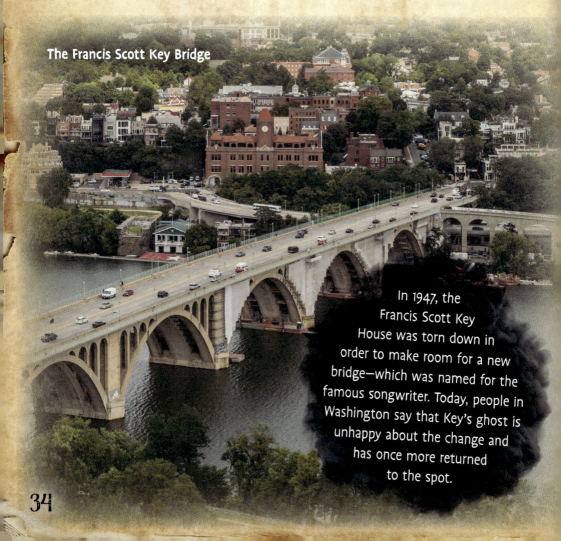

The Francis Scott Key Bridge

In 1947, the Francis Scott Key House was torn down in order to make room for a new bridge—which was named for the famous songwriter. Today, people in Washington say that Key's ghost is unhappy about the change and has once more returned to the spot.

The War of 1812 was a battle between the Americans and the British fought in and around Washington, D.C. During this time, Francis Scott Key was a lawyer living and working in the capital city. He also enjoyed writing poetry. One day near the end of the war, Key witnessed a British attack on Fort McHenry in Baltimore, Maryland. The event—which ended with the American flag still flying—moved him to write the words for "The Star-Spangled Banner." Many years later, in 1931, the song became the national anthem of the United States.

Francis Scott Key

Key's home, built around 1802, was next to the Potomac River in a neighborhood known as Georgetown. In the late 1800s, long after his death, Key is believed to have returned there. Some say it was because the owners were changing the house to make it more modern and up-to-date. Reportedly, loud footsteps, moans, sighs, and even bloodstains on the attic ceiling were signs of the haunting. The spooky events ended only after new owners restored the house to its original style. Had Key's ghost found peace once his home looked as it did when he left it?

The Francis Scott Key House

Phantom Stage

UNIVERSAL STUDIOS
LOS ANGELES, CALIFORNIA

When Universal Studios opened in 1915, the company built and ran the largest movie lot in the world. Universal is still in business today, and people flock to the studio tour, hoping to catch a glimpse of their favorite stars. For years, some were lucky enough to see the ghost of a long-ago star as well.

Universal Studios in 1921

Universal needed a very big lot to film its movies. In fact, it was so big that it could not fit in Hollywood—the movie capital. So, the company built its 230-acre (93-ha) lot a few miles away. With so much space, crews could construct huge sets. One of the most complicated was built on Stage 28 for the 1925 silent film *The Phantom of the Opera*. The movie starred Lon Chaney as the Phantom—a mysterious masked figure who haunts the Paris Opera House.

Lon Chaney as the Phantom

Chaney was truly terrifying as the Phantom. Having grown up with deaf parents, the film star learned at a young age how to express himself through acting. He also created his own makeup for the monsterlike face that the Phantom has under his mask. Sadly, only five years after the movie's release, Chaney died.

After his death, the actor was still often seen on Stage 28, running around the catwalks and wearing the long black cape and mask of his most memorable character. However, the ghostly phantom lost his home when Stage 28 was demolished in 2014. Now, fans wonder where he will appear next.

In 1923, Chaney starred in another silent horror movie called *The Hunchback of Notre Dame*. He created his own terrifying makeup for this character, too.

37

The Lady of the Lake

GREEN-WOOD CEMETERY
BROOKLYN, NEW YORK

Covering nearly 500 rolling acres (200 ha) in Brooklyn is the Green-Wood Cemetery. Dating back to 1838, the cemetery is the final resting place for about 600,000 people. If you look beyond the cemetery's gentle slopes and beautiful trees, you'll discover haunting mysteries buried deep in the ground.

Green-Wood Cemetery

On September 21, 1933, Mabel Smith Douglass was rowing a boat on Lake Placid in upstate New York when she mysteriously disappeared. Soon after she went missing, police began searching for Mabel. They looked and looked but never found her body.

In 1963, about 30 years after Mabel's disappearance, divers made a shocking discovery. They found what looked like a mannequin on the lake's bottom. Upon closer inspection, they saw that the mannequin was actually a perfectly preserved body! When they brought the corpse to the surface, its fragile skin fell apart. Police later determined that the body was that of Mabel Smith Douglass, discovered after years of mystery.

Mabel's body was buried at Green-Wood Cemetery. Today, many believe her tortured spirit walks among the tombstones.

Mabel Smith Douglass worked as a dean at the New Jersey College for Women, which is today a part of Rutgers University. In 1955, the college was renamed Douglass College in her honor.

Home, Sweet Home

THE CUTTS-MADISON HOUSE
WASHINGTON, D.C.

It is often said that ghosts are the spirits of people who are unable to find rest after death. That is not true of the ghost that haunts one home in the nation's capital, however. This famous ghost appears quite comfortable whenever she is seen.

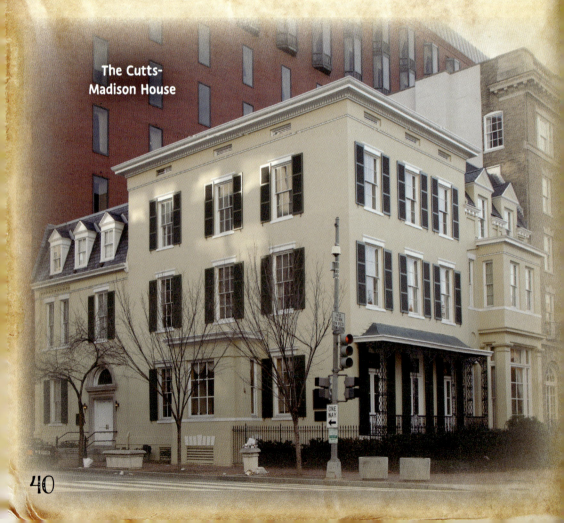

The Cutts-Madison House

Dolley Madison lived a life that was filled with action and drama. In 1809, she moved into the White House with her husband, President James Madison. In 1814, when British troops set fire to the building, the Madisons had to flee and find another home.

Dolley Madison

James Madison died in 1836, and Dolley became a widow. Even though she had once been the First Lady, she struggled to live a comfortable life and pay her bills. In 1837, she moved into the Cutts house, which the Madisons had bought from Richard Cutts, Dolley's brother-in-law. After moving away for a few years to a farm, Dolley returned to the Cutts House in 1843 and lived there until her death in 1849.

Today, the three-story home is known as the Cutts-Madison House. It is also known as the home of Dolley Madison's ghost. At the side of the house, where there used to be a porch, Dolley's ghost has been seen gently rocking in a chair. According to reports, she seems at peace and always greets visitors with a kind and gentle smile.

Dolley Madison's ghost has been part of the city for a very long time. During the second half of the 1800s, members of the Washington Club—a club for businessmen and politicians that was located nearby—would tip their hats to the former First Lady whenever they passed by the house.

Three Morbid Metropolises

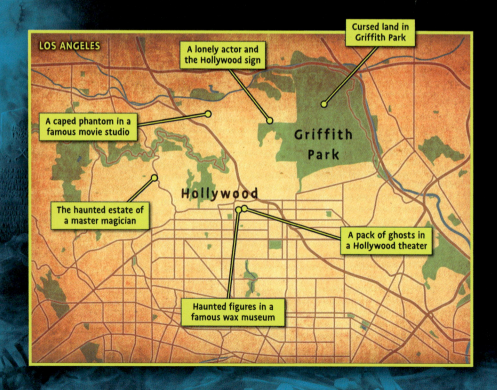

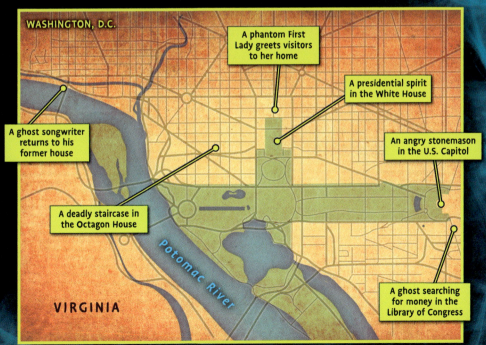

43

Glossary

American Revolution a war fought from 1775 to 1783 in which the American colonies won independence from Great Britain

brownstone a house built using a reddish-brown stone

burial the act of placing a dead body in a grave or tomb

capital the city where a state's or country's government is based

Capitol the building in Washington, D.C., where Congress meets

catwalks narrow walkways above theater stages and seating

celebrities very famous people

Congress the part of the U.S. government that makes laws; Congress is made up of the House of Representatives and the Senate

corpses dead bodies

curse something that brings or causes evil or misfortune

dean the head of a college or university

demolished torn down

dome the rounded top of a building

donated gave as a gift

estate a large property, including land, a house, and sometimes other buildings

gardenias white flowers with a strong, sweet smell

grief great sadness

grim gloomy and unpleasant

House of Representatives one of the two main groups that make laws for the United States

inheritance property received from someone upon that person's death

lavish generous or extravagant

legend a story that is handed down from the past that may be based on fact but is not always completely true

lurking secretly hiding

lyrics the words to a song

mannequin a life-size model of a human being

mansion a very large house

monstrous horrible or frightening

national anthem the official song of a country

outbreak the sudden spread of a disease among a group of people

paranormal events that can't be explained by science

phantom a ghost or spirit

preserved kept in good condition

projectionist a person who operates the machines that show films in a theater

public square an open space in a city or town where people gather

reels spools of things, such as film

restored brought something back to its original condition

rival someone who is competing against another person

séances gatherings for the purpose of communicating with ghosts

Senate one of the two main groups that make laws for the United States

silent film a movie in which there is no recorded sound

smallpox a disease that causes high fever and can be deadly

spirits supernatural creatures, such as ghosts

stonemason someone who works with bricks and stone

supernatural something unusual that breaks the laws of nature

tortured caused extreme pain or suffering

typhoid a disease that causes fever, weakness, and headaches

unnerving unsettling or scary

usher someone who shows people to their seats in a theater

vowed promised oneself something

War of 1812 a war fought from 1812 to 1815 between the United States and Great Britain, largely over control of waterways and shipping routes

wings sections that are attached to the main part of a building

45

Read More

Gitlin, Marty. *Investigating Octavia Spencer's Haunted House (The Haunted Experiences of Celebrities)*. Hallandale, FL: Mitchell Lane Publishers, 2025.

Lunis, Natalie and Sarah Parvis. *Startling Stay: Scary Hotels and Inns (Where You Dare Not Go)*. Minneapolis: Bearport Publishing Company, 2025.

Mihaly, Christy. *The Haunted History of Washington, DC (Haunted History of the United States)*. North Mankato, MN: ABDO Publishing, 2024.

Learn More Online

1. Go to **FactSurfer.com** or scan the QR code below.

2. Enter "**Morbid Metropolis**" into the search box.

3. Click on the cover of this book to see a list of websites.

Index

Bartell, Jan Bryant 9
Belasco, David 26-27
Belasco Theatre 26-27
Brown, James 21
Capitol building 23
Chaney, Lon 37
Churchill, Winston 11
Cutts-Madison House 40-41
Cutts, Richard 40-41
Dakota, the 14-15
Douglass, Mabel Smith 39
Ear Inn 20-21
Entwistle, Peg 7
Francis Scott Key House and Bridge 34-35
Green-Wood Cemetery 38-39
Griffith, Griffith J. 18-19, 42
Griffith Park 18-19, 42
Hollywood, California 6-7, 12-13, 18, 24-25, 30-31, 37
Hollywood sign 6-7, 18
Houdini, Harry 24-25
House of Death 8-9
Key, Francis Scott 34-35
L'Enfant, Pierre Charles 17
Lennon, John 15
Library of Congress 22-23, 43
Lincoln, Abraham 10-11
Lincoln, Mary 10-11
Lincoln, Willie 10-11
Los Angeles, California 6, 18, 24, 30, 36, 42

Madison, Dolley 41
Madison, James 41
Monroe, Marilyn 31
movies 7, 12, 24, 31, 37
New York, New York 8, 14, 20, 26, 32
Octagon House 28-29, 43
Ono, Yoko 15
Petronilla, Doña 19
Phantom of the Opera 31, 37
Price, Vincent 31
Rutgers University 39
Tayloe, John 29
Twain, Mark 9
United States House of Representatives 16-17
United States Senate 16-17
Universal Studios 36
Vogue Theatre 12-13
War of 1812 35
Washington, D.C. 4, 10-11, 16-17, 22, 28, 34-35, 40, 43
Washington, George 17, 21, 29
Washington Square Park 32-33
White House 10-11, 28, 41, 43

47

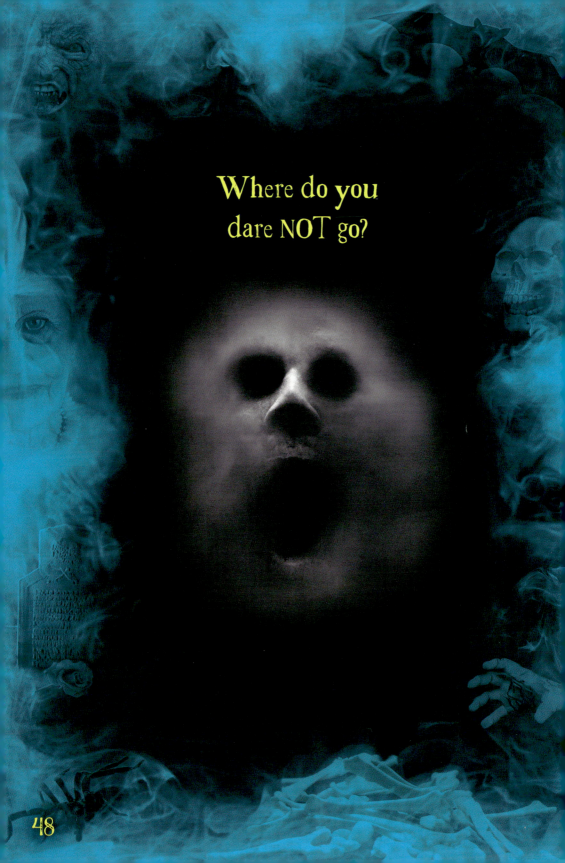